THE NOVEL WRITING BLUEPRINT

A STEP-BY-STEP NOVEL PLANNING WORKBOOK

DARK GROVE PRESS

The Novel Writing Blueprint
A Step-By-Step Novel Planning Workbook

ISBN: 978-1-7387711-3-4 (paperback)

TABLE OF CONTENTS

TABLE OF CONTENTS

INTRODUCTION

The Novel Writing Blueprint is aimed at helping writers find an exciting story idea, plan and organize the story plot, create realistic and interesting characters, and delve fully into their story world so they can get to complete the first draft.

HOW TO USE THIS WORKBOOK

The Novel Writing Blueprint uses the elements of fiction to take writers through each step of the fiction planning process:

- Brainstorm story ideas
- Use story conflict for plot ideas
- Follow a plot structure
- Create characters
- Create the setting & world
- Choose the point of view
- Deepen the story with theme, mood, and tone
- Brainstorm scene ideas
- Create a scene list
- Outline each story scene
- Write the first draft

Starting from page one, *The Novel Writing Blueprint* guides the writer through their story creation with prompts and templates. By the end of the workbook, the writer will have their entire novel planned and their first draft completed.

NOTES

PART I

IDEAS

IN THIS SECTION

STORY INSPIRATION

IDEAS BRAINSTORM

EXPAND THE IDEA

"If you stuff yourself full of poems, essays, plays, stories, novels, films, comic strips, magazines, music, you automatically explode every morning like Old Faithful.

I have never had a dry spell in my life, mainly because I feed myself well, to the point of bursting.

I wake early and hear my morning voices leaping around in my head like jumping beans. I get out of bed quickly, to trap them before they escape."

- RAY BRADBURY

INSPIRATION

Consider the things that inspire you creatively - this can be tv, movies, books, travel, hobbies - when you are in need of inspiration, come back to this page.

BOOKS THAT INSPIRE CREATIVITY:

TV AND MOVIES THAT INSPIRE CREATIVITY:

ACTIVITIES AND HOBBIES THAT INSPIRE CREATIVITY:

IDEAS BRAINSTORM

Keep track of story ideas below

IDEA:

IDEA:

IDEA:

IDEAS BRAINSTORM

IDEA:

IDEA:

IDEA:

IDEAS BRAINSTORM

IDEA:

IDEA:

IDEA:

IDEAS BRAINSTORM

IDEA:

IDEA:

IDEA:

IDEAS BRAINSTORM

IDEA:

IDEA:

IDEA:

IDEAS BRAINSTORM

IDEA:

IDEA:

IDEA:

EXPAND THE IDEA #1

Using an idea from one of the previous pages, expand on the story

PLOT: WHAT HAPPENS

CHARACTERS: WHO IT HAPPENS TO

EXPAND THE IDEA #1

SETTING: WHERE THE STORY TAKES PLACE

POINT OF VIEW: HOW THE STORY IS TOLD

THEME: THE DEEPER MEANING

TONE & MOOD OF THE STORY

EXPAND THE IDEA #2

Using an idea from one of the previous pages, expand on the story

PLOT: WHAT HAPPENS

CHARACTERS: WHO IT HAPPENS TO

EXPAND THE IDEA #2

SETTING: WHERE THE STORY TAKES PLACE

POINT OF VIEW: HOW THE STORY IS TOLD

THEME: THE DEEPER MEANING

TONE & MOOD OF THE STORY

EXPAND THE IDEA #3

Using an idea from one of the previous pages, expand on the story

PLOT: WHAT HAPPENS

CHARACTERS: WHO IT HAPPENS TO

EXPAND THE IDEA #3

SETTING: WHERE THE STORY TAKES PLACE

POINT OF VIEW: HOW THE STORY IS TOLD

THEME: THE DEEPER MEANING

TONE & MOOD OF THE STORY

EXPAND THE IDEA #4

Using an idea from one of the previous pages, expand on the story

PLOT: WHAT HAPPENS

CHARACTERS: WHO IT HAPPENS TO

EXPAND THE IDEA #4

SETTING: WHERE THE STORY TAKES PLACE

POINT OF VIEW: HOW THE STORY IS TOLD

THEME: THE DEEPER MEANING

TONE & MOOD OF THE STORY

EXPAND THE IDEA #5

Using an idea from one of the previous pages, expand on the story

PLOT: WHAT HAPPENS

CHARACTERS: WHO IT HAPPENS TO

EXPAND THE IDEA #5

SETTING: WHERE THE STORY TAKES PLACE

POINT OF VIEW: HOW THE STORY IS TOLD

THEME: THE DEEPER MEANING

TONE & MOOD OF THE STORY

EXPAND THE IDEA #6

Using an idea from one of the previous pages, expand on the story

PLOT: WHAT HAPPENS

CHARACTERS: WHO IT HAPPENS TO

EXPAND THE IDEA #6

SETTING: WHERE THE STORY TAKES PLACE

POINT OF VIEW: HOW THE STORY IS TOLD

THEME: THE DEEPER MEANING

TONE & MOOD OF THE STORY

EXPAND THE IDEA #7

Using an idea from one of the previous pages, expand on the story

PLOT: WHAT HAPPENS

CHARACTERS: WHO IT HAPPENS TO

EXPAND THE IDEA #7

SETTING: WHERE THE STORY TAKES PLACE

POINT OF VIEW: HOW THE STORY IS TOLD

THEME: THE DEEPER MEANING

TONE & MOOD OF THE STORY

EXPAND THE IDEA #8

Using an idea from one of the previous pages, expand on the story

PLOT: WHAT HAPPENS

CHARACTERS: WHO IT HAPPENS TO

EXPAND THE IDEA #8

SETTING: WHERE THE STORY TAKES PLACE

POINT OF VIEW: HOW THE STORY IS TOLD

THEME: THE DEEPER MEANING

TONE & MOOD OF THE STORY

EXPAND THE IDEA #9

Using an idea from one of the previous pages, expand on the story

PLOT: WHAT HAPPENS

CHARACTERS: WHO IT HAPPENS TO

EXPAND THE IDEA #9

SETTING: WHERE THE STORY TAKES PLACE

POINT OF VIEW: HOW THE STORY IS TOLD

THEME: THE DEEPER MEANING

TONE & MOOD OF THE STORY

EXPAND THE IDEA #10

Using an idea from one of the previous pages, expand on the story

PLOT: WHAT HAPPENS

CHARACTERS: WHO IT HAPPENS TO

EXPAND THE IDEA #10

SETTING: WHERE THE STORY TAKES PLACE

POINT OF VIEW: HOW THE STORY IS TOLD

THEME: THE DEEPER MEANING

TONE & MOOD OF THE STORY

PART II

STORY PREP

IN THIS SECTION

CONFLICT

PLOT STRUCTURE

CHARACTER

SETTING & WORLDBUILDING

POINT OF VIEW

THEME, MOOD & TONE

PREPARING STORY ELEMENTS

Writing a novel can be intimidating because there are so many factors to think about when crafting a story. One way to counteract this overwhelm is by planning each element of the story first, before the writing process begins.

This section of the workbook is the largest, where we will look at each story element on its own, easing the process of planning story scenes later on.

Those who have already written their story will also benefit from this section by having the structure to organize their story world and detangle their plot or characters.

This section starts off with looking at story conflict before moving into plot structure. Next is creating characters, followed by setting and worldbuilding. Finally, we will look at deepening the story's meaning through theme, mood, and tone.

CONFLICT

CONFLICT

WHAT IS LITERARY CONFLICT?

Conflict is a literary element that creates obstacles or challenges for the characters within a story to overcome, thus building suspense, intriguing readers, and moving the plot forward.

A story without conflict is a story without tension or intrigue. Conflict occurs when something is in opposition with a character, thus creating an obstacle to overcome.

Conflict can be something small (*a disagreement with another character*) or something major (*a massive war between kingdoms*), but without challenges for the characters to face, there is no story to tell.

Use the types of conflict outlined below to spark ideas for conflict within your story.

TYPES OF STORY CONFLICT
Character vs Character
Character vs Self
Character vs Society
Character vs Nature
Character vs Supernatural
Character vs Fate
Character vs Technology

CONFLICT

Use the following types of conflict in fiction to help create ideas for plot points within your story

CHARACTER VS. CHARACTER
the characters within the story have opposing desires, beliefs, or goals, creating tension between them; these characters are unable to coexist peacefully *hero vs villain; protagonist vs antagonist* <u>story example:</u> Harry Potter vs Voldemort in the *Harry Potter* series

CHARACTER VS. SELF
the character experiences an internal struggle; this can be self-doubt that needs to be overcome, a moral dilemma, a choice that must be made; a clash between what the character wants and what they need *protagonist's internal conflict* <u>story example:</u> Prince Hamlet's internal struggle in *Hamlet*

CHARACTER VS. SOCIETY
the character lives within an oppressive system, dealing with corruption and injustice from the world around them *protagonist vs government* <u>story example:</u> Katniss Everdeen vs The Capitol in *The Hunger Games*

CONFLICT

Use the following types of conflict in fiction to help create ideas for plot points within your story

CHARACTER VS. NATURE

the character struggles to survive in the face of deadly wildlife, natural disasters, or a post-apocalyptic landscape

human vs wild animal; human vs avalanche

story example: Hugh Glass vs the wilderness (and a vicious bear) in *The Revenant*

CHARACTER VS. SUPERNATURAL

the character battles against paranormal entities like ghosts, demons, monsters, and other creatures of the occult

human vs demon

story example: Bella Swan vs the vampires in *Twilight*

CHARACTER VS. FATE

the character fights against a prophecy, oracle, or prediction

person vs destiny

story example: Oedipus vs the prophecy in *Oedipus Rex*

CHARACTER VS. TECHNOLOGY

the character fights against technology that has become too powerful or is being used for nefarious reasons

person vs smart house; person vs robot; person vs experiment

story example: Dr. Frankenstein's creation in *Frankenstein*

CONFLICT BRAINSTORM

What obstacles will the characters in your story face that can act as intriguing plot points and twists?

CONFLICT BRAINSTORM

CONFLICT BRAINSTORM

CONFLICT BRAINSTORM

CONFLICT BRAINSTORM

PLOT

PLOT

WHAT IS LITERARY CONFLICT?

The sequence of events, following a cause-and-effect pattern, through which the story develops and unfolds.

THE WHAT

The plot is the "what" of the story - what happens?

When describing a story's major events (describing what happens) we are describing the plot of the book.

EVERY WHAT NEEDS A WHY

While the plot of the story is the "what", every "what" needs a logical "why". A plot should not be a senseless series of random events - the actions and reactions of the characters in the story should be moving and directing the plot whenever possible.

TYPES OF PLOT STRUCTURES

There are countless numbers of plot structures that one could use to help structure their story. The following pages make use of three different plot structures:

FREYTAG'S PYRAMID

THREE-ACT STRUCTURE

SEVEN-POINT PLOT STRUCTURE

STORY PLOT

Choose one of the plot structures below to plan out the plot points of your story

STRUCTURE: FREYTAG'S PYRAMID
Exposition
Rising Action
Climax
Falling Action
Resolution

STRUCTURE: THREE-ACT STRUCTURE		
	ACT I: THE SETUP	
Exposition	Inciting Incident	Plot Point 1
	ACT II: THE CONFRONTATION	
Rising Action	Midpoint	Plot Point 2
	ACT III: THE RESOLUTION	
Pre-Climax	Climax	Denouement

STRUCTURE: SEVEN-POINT PLOT STRUCTURE
The Hook
Plot Point 1
Pinch Point 1
Midpoint
Pinch Point 2
Plot Point 2
Resolution

FREYTAG'S PYRAMID

This plot structure involves looking at the events of the story in five stages: exposition, rising action, climax, falling action, and resolution

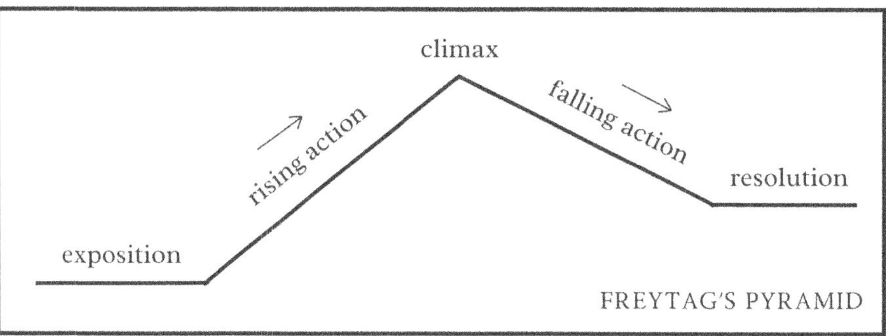

STAGE 1: EXPOSITION
• introduces the setting and the characters • has a focus on building the story world and getting the reader attached to the main character(s) • set the tone and mood of the story

STAGE 2: RISING ACTION
• introduction to the antagonistic force and the stakes of the story • protagonist's reaction to arising obstacles • meeting new allies or enemies

STAGE 3: CLIMAX
• the peak of the conflict; a major turning point • this event causes a change in the main character • the protagonist must now move from reaction into action

FREYTAG'S PYRAMID

STAGE 4: FALLING ACTION

- the aftermath or consequences of the climax
- emergence of character growth from overcoming the obstacles that occured throughout the story
- beginning to tie up loose story threads

STAGE 5: RESOLUTION

- the conflicts of the story are now resolved
- the character experiences a "new normal" and are forever changed from the events of the story

PLOT SUMMARY

Using the five stages of this plot structure, summarize the main plot event that occurs in each section

FREYTAG'S PYRAMID OUTLINE

Expand on the story events and obstacles for each stage

STAGE 1: EXPOSITION

FREYTAG'S PYRAMID OUTLINE

STAGE 1: EXPOSITION

FREYTAG'S PYRAMID OUTLINE

Expand on the story events and obstacles for each stage

STAGE 2: RISING ACTION

FREYTAG'S PYRAMID OUTLINE

STAGE 2: RISING ACTION

FREYTAG'S PYRAMID OUTLINE

Expand on the story events and obstacles for each stage

STAGE 3: CLIMAX

FREYTAG'S PYRAMID OUTLINE

STAGE 3: CLIMAX

FREYTAG'S PYRAMID OUTLINE

Expand on the story events and obstacles for each stage

STAGE 4: FALLING ACTION

FREYTAG'S PYRAMID OUTLINE

STAGE 4: FALLING ACTION

FREYTAG'S PYRAMID OUTLINE

Expand on the story events and obstacles for each stage

STAGE 5: RESOLUTION

FREYTAG'S PYRAMID OUTLINE

STAGE 5: RESOLUTION

THREE-ACT STRUCTURE

This plot structure splits the story into three acts: (1) the setup, (2) the confrontation, and (3) the resolution; each act contains three major plot elements

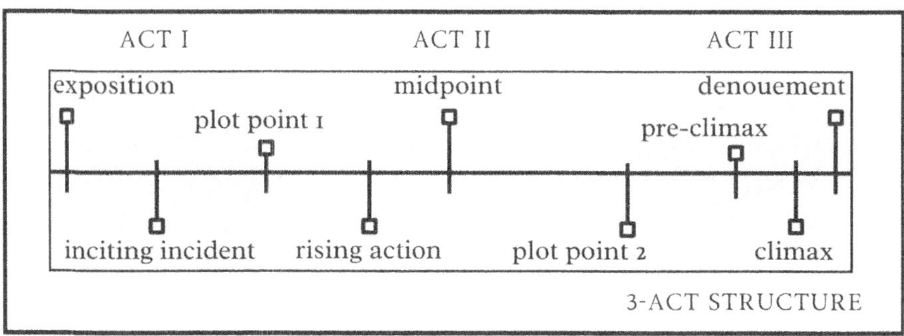

ACT I: THE SETUP	
EXPOSITION	*introduction to the character and their "normal world"*
INCITING INCIDENT	*the first hint at the main story's conflict*
PLOT POINT 1	*main character enters through the door of no return*

ACT II: THE CONFRONTATION	
RISING ACTION	*character has entered into a strange new world, dealing with new obstacles, new allies, and new enemies*
MIDPOINT	*a plot twist or major setback raises the stakes*
PLOT POINT 2	*character moves from reactive to proactive, building confidence*

ACT III: THE RESOLUTION	
PRE-CLIMAX	*character faces their biggest setback yet; their darkest moment where all feels lost*
CLIMAX	*character uses everything they've learned from overcoming the obstacles in the story to finally defeat the antagonist*
DENOUEMENT	*loose ends are tied up; the happily ever after*

THREE-ACT STRUCTURE

exposition, inciting incident, plot point 1

ACT I: THE SETUP

THREE-ACT STRUCTURE

ACT I: THE SETUP

THREE-ACT STRUCTURE

rising action, midpoint, plot point 2

ACT II: THE CONFRONTATION

ACT II: THE CONFRONTATION

THREE-ACT STRUCTURE

pre-climax, climax, denouement

ACT III: THE RESOLUTION

THREE-ACT STRUCTURE

ACT III: THE RESOLUTION

7-POINT STORY STRUCTURE

This plot structure involves seven major plot points that pull the reader through the story

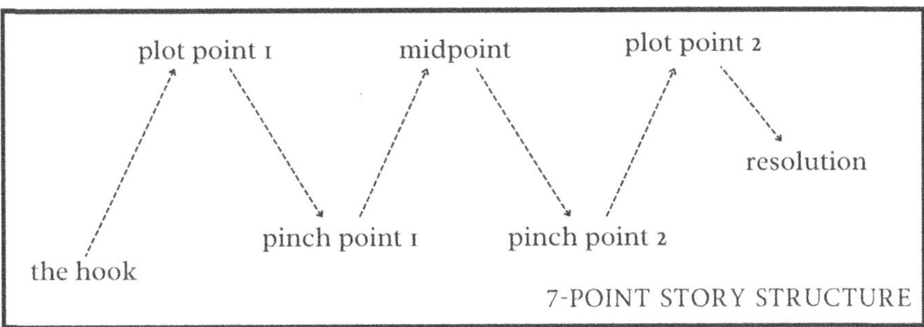

THE HOOK
pulls the reader into the story; introduces the characters and the story world

PLOT POINT 1
an event pushes the character outside of their comfort zone, starting the main storyline

PINCH POINT 1
first encounter with the antagonistic force stakes are raised; foreshadowing of what's to come

MIDPOINT
plot twist that causes the character to step into a more active role in preparing to defeat the antagonist

PINCH POINT 2
failure leads the character to their darkest moment seeming moment of defeat

7-POINT STORY STRUCTURE

This plot structure involves seven major plot points that pull the reader through the story

PLOT POINT 2
character has the final piece of information and/or skills to defeat the antagonist

RESOLUTION
the antagonist has been defeated and the conflict of the story is resolved

PLOT SUMMARY

Following the seven plot points, summarize the main events of the story

7-POINT STORY STRUCTURE

7-POINT STORY STRUCTURE

THE HOOK

PLOT POINT 1

PINCH POINT 1

7-POINT STORY STRUCTURE

MIDPOINT

PINCH POINT 2

7-POINT STORY STRUCTURE

PLOT POINT 2

RESOLUTION

CHARACTER

CHARACTER LIST

Consider which characters are needed to help tell the story and what narrative role they will play

CHARACTER:
STORY ROLE:

CHARACTER:
STORY ROLE:

CHARACTER:
STORY ROLE:

CHARACTER:
STORY ROLE:

CHARACTER:
STORY ROLE:

CHARACTER LIST

Consider which characters are needed to help tell the story and what narrative role they will play

CHARACTER:
STORY ROLE:

CHARACTER:
STORY ROLE:

CHARACTER:
STORY ROLE:

CHARACTER:
STORY ROLE:

CHARACTER:
STORY ROLE:

CHARACTER RELATIONSHIPS

Use the space below to list the characters and how they are connected; this can be a family tree, a mindmap, or any other way of organizing character relationships

CHARACTER QUESTIONS

On the following pages, outline more about the story characters

For each primary character, consider:

- *how does this character's action, or inaction, help to progress the plot?*
- *what is this character's backstory and how have these experiences shaped their personality?*
- *what are this character's personal goals and desires?*
- *how might the goals of this character clash with the goals of other characters in the story?*

CHARACTER DEEP DIVE

CHARACTER:

PHYSICAL ATTRIBUTES:

BACKSTORY:

GOALS & PERSONALITY:

CHARACTER DEEP DIVE

CHARACTER:
PHYSICAL ATTRIBUTES:
BACKSTORY:
GOALS & PERSONALITY:

CHARACTER DEEP DIVE

CHARACTER:

PHYSICAL ATTRIBUTES:

BACKSTORY:

GOALS & PERSONALITY:

CHARACTER DEEP DIVE

CHARACTER:

PHYSICAL ATTRIBUTES:

BACKSTORY:

GOALS & PERSONALITY:

CHARACTER DEEP DIVE

CHARACTER:

PHYSICAL ATTRIBUTES:

BACKSTORY:

GOALS & PERSONALITY:

CHARACTER DEEP DIVE

CHARACTER:

PHYSICAL ATTRIBUTES:

BACKSTORY:

GOALS & PERSONALITY:

CHARACTER DEEP DIVE

CHARACTER:

PHYSICAL ATTRIBUTES:

BACKSTORY:

GOALS & PERSONALITY:

CHARACTER DEEP DIVE

CHARACTER:
PHYSICAL ATTRIBUTES:
BACKSTORY:
GOALS & PERSONALITY:

CHARACTER DEEP DIVE

CHARACTER:
PHYSICAL ATTRIBUTES:
BACKSTORY:
GOALS & PERSONALITY:

CHARACTER DEEP DIVE

CHARACTER:

PHYSICAL ATTRIBUTES:

BACKSTORY:

GOALS & PERSONALITY:

SETTING & WORLDBUILDING

SETTING LIST

Outline ideas for story setting and scene locations; include any notable physical details that should stay consistent from scene to scene (i.e., a red couch in the coffee shop), or any ideas for character moments in that location

LOCATION:

LOCATION:

LOCATION:

SETTING LIST

LOCATION:

LOCATION:

LOCATION:

LOCATION:

SETTING LIST

LOCATION:

LOCATION:

LOCATION:

LOCATION:

SETTING LIST

LOCATION:

LOCATION:

LOCATION:

LOCATION:

WORLDBUILDING

For some story types (i.e., historical fiction or fantasy) the setting is an important factor that provides context to the story itself; use these pages for stories that require more intensive worldbuilding

Use the space below to draw a rough outline of a map, floor plan, or anything that will help you to visualize the story setting

WORLDBUILDING QUESTIONS

Use the following questions to plan out your story's world

- *what are some key features of this location and its people?*
- *what are the different groups of people in this location?*
- *what are the common beliefs or perspectives of people in this location and how would that affect the story being told?*
- *how do the rules and standards of this culture affect the geography of this location (i.e., historical landmarks, churches, schools, urban setting, farms)*
- *what is the history or lore of this location?*

WORLDBUILDING

LOCATION

HISTORY

GEOGRAPHY

CULTURE

OTHER FEATURES

WORLDBUILDING

LOCATION

HISTORY

GEOGRAPHY

CULTURE

OTHER FEATURES

WORLDBUILDING

LOCATION
HISTORY
GEOGRAPHY
CULTURE
OTHER FEATURES

WORLDBUILDING

LOCATION

HISTORY

GEOGRAPHY

CULTURE

OTHER FEATURES

WORLDBUILDING

LOCATION

HISTORY

GEOGRAPHY

CULTURE

OTHER FEATURES

WORLDBUILDING

LOCATION

HISTORY

GEOGRAPHY

CULTURE

OTHER FEATURES

POINT OF VIEW

POINT OF VIEW

The point of view is the lens through which the story is told and effects how the story is perceived by the reader

FIRST PERSON POV

The narrator tells the story from their own perspective

Uses *I, my, we, us*

My heart leaped in my chest as I walked down the dark hallway

Examples of First-Person Narratives:

Rebecca by Daphne du Maurier

The Martian by Andy Weir

SECOND PERSON POV

The narrator addresses the reader directly

Uses *you, your, yourself*

Your heart leaps in your chest as you walk down the dark hallway

Examples featuring Second-Person Narratives:

The Fifth Season by N.K. Jemisin

The Night Circus by Erin Morgenstern

THIRD PERSON POV

The narrator exists outside of the story, following multiple characters and describing their experiences

Uses *he, she, they*

Her heart leaped in her chest as she walked down the dark hallway

Examples of Third-Person Narratives:

Pride and Prejudice by Jane Austen

Mistborn by Brandon Sanderson

POINT OF VIEW

Third person can be further split into two categories: (1) omniscient, and (2) limited

THIRD PERSON OMNISCIENT

The narrator has an all-knowing perspective and is able to dive into the thoughts and feelings of every character, while also knowing past, present, and future events that they may foreshadow to the reader

THIRD PERSON LIMITED

The narrator only knows what the current viewpoint character knows; they do not know the secrets, thoughts, or feelings of other characters in the story unless those things are directly shared with the viewpoint character, or the viewpoint character is making assumptions based off their own observations

VIEWPOINT SUMMARY

Consider which perspective would be best used to tell your story, the most common being first and third person point of view

FIRST PERSON	Uses *I, my, me, we, us*
SECOND PERSON	Uses *you, your, yourself*
THIRD PERSON	Uses *he, she, her, him, they*
LIMITED *narrator knows only what the character knows*	OMNISCIENT *narrator is all-knowing*

VIEWPOINT EXPERIMENT

To decide which point of view works best for you/your story, use the following pages to write a scene, sampling each point of view and consider which feels best for your story

FIRST PERSON

Use this page to experiment with point of view by writing a scene from first person perspective

SECOND PERSON

Use this page to experiment with point of view by writing a scene from second person perspective

THIRD PERSON

Use this page to experiment with point of view by writing a scene from third person perspective

CHOOSING A POV

When deciding which point of view to choose, consider the following strengths and weaknesses of each

FIRST PERSON

STRENGTHS	WEAKNESSES
• Easier perspective to write as a newer writer • Allows reader to more easily connect to the character • Clearly see the thoughts and motivations of the viewpoint character	• Only able to deeply see into the thoughts and feelings of one character • Can be disorienting for the reader to change to other viewpoint characters in a story with dual points of view

SECOND PERSON

STRENGTHS	WEAKNESSES
• Unique reader experience that can provide a sense of surrealism for the reader	• Most difficult viewpoint to do effectively for a full-length novel

THIRD PERSON

STRENGTHS	WEAKNESSES
• Smoother transition for the reader when switching between multiple points of view • Able to show the feelings and motivations of every character (third omniscient)	• Can be challenging for the reader to connect with the viewpoint character • Only able to deeply see the thoughts and feelings of one character (third limited)

CHOOSE YOUR POINT OF VIEW

☐ FIRST PERSON

☐ SECOND PERSON

☐ THIRD PERSON

OMNISCIENT OR LIMITED

CHOOSING A POV CHARACTER

The point of view is the lens through which the story is told, making the point of view character an important storytelling decision; consider which character(s) might work best based on their personality and connection to the story

THEME,
MOOD & TONE

THEME

Theme is the central idea or meaning behind a story;
a story's theme provides commentary on a universal concept

EXAMPLES OF STORY THEME

forgiveness	revenge
love	survival
power	corruption

THE THEMATIC STATEMENT

by expanding on the themes above, we can create the story's thematic statement

theme: *revenge*

thematic statements: *revenge is a deserved result of injustice*

the pursual of revenge can have negative consequences for everyone involved

getting revenge will not make someone happy

IMPORTANCE OF THEME

a story's theme allows the reader to relate to the experiences of the character, even without having been in that same exact situation

a reader of fantasy will not have the experience of going on a quest and facing mortal dangers like in *The Lord of the Rings*, but they can relate to the themes of *found family* and *good versus evil* seen throughout the story, which help readers empathize and bond with the characters

THEME

Use the following questions to consider the deeper meaning of your story and better identify the theme

WHAT IS THE MAIN CHARACTER'S BIGGEST STRUGGLE TO OVERCOME IN THE STORY?

IS THERE A BELIEF YOUR MAIN CHARACTER HOLDS THAT GUIDES MANY OF THEIR ACTIONS?

WHAT IS THE MAIN LESSON YOUR CHARACTER LEARNS BY THE END OF THE BOOK?

THEME

Consider the bigger picture of your story

WHAT ARE THE MAIN THINGS THAT HAPPEN IN THE STORY WHICH IMPACT THE CHARACTER AND THE DIRECTION OF THE PLOT?

BRAINSTORM IDEAS FOR THE STORY'S THEME

MOOD & TONE

Mood and tone can often overlap in a story and should compliment one another

TONE IN STORY

the story's tone is the writer's approach to the story which is expressed through the writing

for example, a story with a *suspenseful tone*, would come from the writer withholding information from the reader

a *humorous tone* would come from a writer taking a light-hearted approach and using a comedic lens to tell the story

MOOD IN STORY

the mood is the feeling that the story evokes within the reader, which can change from scene to scene

a story following a character going through grief or depression could take on a *gloomy* or *melancholic mood*

an uplifting story where good things happen more often than bad could result in a *cheerful* or *optimistic mood*

TONE & MOOD

analyze the tone and mood of the story by considering:

how does the character approach life and view their circumstances? (i.e., are they sarcastic, optimistic, depressed, cynical, etc.)

what do you want the reader to feel while reading your story? (i.e., joyful, shocked, uneasy, excited, etc.)

is your goal to highlight the beauty of, or the tragedies within, the human experience? (i.e., working towards a happy ending or a dark but "realistic" ending)

MOOD & TONE

Use the questions on the last page to brainstorm the mood and tone of your story

MOOD & TONE

Use the questions on the last page to brainstorm the mood and tone of your story

MOOD & TONE

Use the questions on the last page to brainstorm the mood and tone of your story

PART III

SCENES

IN THIS SECTION

SCENE BRAINSTORM

SCENE LIST

SCENE OUTLINE

BALANCING SCENES

Novels are made up of units of story known as scenes; each scene should have a beginning, middle, and end, and should work to either serve the plot, or deepen our knowledge of characters or the story world

There are two types of scenes: (1) action scenes, and (2) sequels

ACTION SCENES

this type of scene shows us a character in a state of action; this could include a scene where the characters are planning, arguing, escaping, investigating, or any number of actions

SEQUELS

this type of scene shows us a character in a state of reaction; these are scenes that serve to reveal more about the characters background or about the worldbuilding; these scenes involve the character contemplating a choice, processing an event, reflect on past circumstances, and many more

To have a well-rounded novel that reaches readers on an emotional level, ensure that there is a balance between action scenes and sequels (scenes of reflection)

SCENE BRAINSTORM

Use the following pages to make note of any ideas for scenes that sound exciting or that are pivotal to the story

SCENE IDEA

SCENE IDEA

SCENE IDEA

SCENE BRAINSTORM

SCENE IDEA

SCENE IDEA

SCENE IDEA

SCENE BRAINSTORM

SCENE IDEA

SCENE IDEA

SCENE IDEA

SCENE BRAINSTORM

SCENE IDEA

SCENE IDEA

SCENE IDEA

SCENE BRAINSTORM

SCENE IDEA

SCENE IDEA

SCENE IDEA

SCENE BRAINSTORM

SCENE IDEA

SCENE IDEA

SCENE IDEA

SCENE LIST

Use the plotting pages and the scene pages from previous to plan out the story's order of events including a brief summary of each chapter/scene.

When planning the order of events, consider the pace of the story:

How far apart are the story's major plot points?
Is there a balance between the action of the story and the emotion of the story?

SCENE:

SCENE:

SCENE LIST

SCENE:

SCENE:

SCENE:

SCENE LIST

SCENE:

SCENE:

SCENE:

SCENE LIST

SCENE:

SCENE:

SCENE:

SCENE LIST

SCENE:

SCENE:

SCENE:

SCENE LIST

SCENE:

SCENE:

SCENE:

SCENE LIST

SCENE:

SCENE:

SCENE:

SCENE LIST

SCENE:

SCENE:

SCENE:

SCENE LIST

SCENE:

SCENE:

SCENE:

SCENE LIST

SCENE:

SCENE:

SCENE:

SCENE LIST

SCENE:

SCENE:

SCENE:

SCENE LIST

SCENE:

SCENE:

SCENE:

SCENE LIST

SCENE:

SCENE:

SCENE:

SCENE LIST

SCENE:

SCENE:

SCENE:

SCENE OUTLINE

Using the scene list from the previous pages, dive deeper into each scene in the following pages

SCENE
SCENE CHARACTERS
SCENE SETTING & LOCATIONS
SCENE OUTLINE

SCENE

CHARACTERS

SETTING & LOCATIONS

SCENE OUTLINE

SCENE

CHARACTERS

SETTING & LOCATIONS

SCENE OUTLINE

SCENE

CHARACTERS

SETTING & LOCATIONS

SCENE OUTLINE

SCENE
CHARACTERS
SETTING & LOCATIONS
SCENE OUTLINE

SCENE

CHARACTERS

SETTING & LOCATIONS

SCENE OUTLINE

SCENE

CHARACTERS

SETTING & LOCATIONS

SCENE OUTLINE

SCENE

CHARACTERS

SETTING & LOCATIONS

SCENE OUTLINE

SCENE

CHARACTERS

SETTING & LOCATIONS

SCENE OUTLINE

SCENE
CHARACTERS
SETTING & LOCATIONS
SCENE OUTLINE

SCENE
CHARACTERS
SETTING & LOCATIONS
SCENE OUTLINE

SCENE

CHARACTERS

SETTING & LOCATIONS

SCENE OUTLINE

SCENE

CHARACTERS

SETTING & LOCATIONS

SCENE OUTLINE

SCENE

CHARACTERS

SETTING & LOCATIONS

SCENE OUTLINE

SCENE

CHARACTERS

SETTING & LOCATIONS

SCENE OUTLINE

SCENE

CHARACTERS

SETTING & LOCATIONS

SCENE OUTLINE

SCENE

CHARACTERS

SETTING & LOCATIONS

SCENE OUTLINE

SCENE
CHARACTERS
SETTING & LOCATIONS
SCENE OUTLINE

SCENE
CHARACTERS
SETTING & LOCATIONS
SCENE OUTLINE

SCENE
CHARACTERS
SETTING & LOCATIONS
SCENE OUTLINE

SCENE

CHARACTERS

SETTING & LOCATIONS

SCENE OUTLINE

SCENE
CHARACTERS
SETTING & LOCATIONS
SCENE OUTLINE

SCENE
CHARACTERS
SETTING & LOCATIONS
SCENE OUTLINE

SCENE
CHARACTERS
SETTING & LOCATIONS
SCENE OUTLINE

SCENE

CHARACTERS

SETTING & LOCATIONS

SCENE OUTLINE

SCENE

CHARACTERS

SETTING & LOCATIONS

SCENE OUTLINE

SCENE

CHARACTERS

SETTING & LOCATIONS

SCENE OUTLINE

SCENE

CHARACTERS

SETTING & LOCATIONS

SCENE OUTLINE

SCENE

CHARACTERS

SETTING & LOCATIONS

SCENE OUTLINE

SCENE

CHARACTERS

SETTING & LOCATIONS

SCENE OUTLINE

SCENE
CHARACTERS
SETTING & LOCATIONS
SCENE OUTLINE

SCENE

CHARACTERS

SETTING & LOCATIONS

SCENE OUTLINE

SCENE

CHARACTERS

SETTING & LOCATIONS

SCENE OUTLINE

SCENE

CHARACTERS

SETTING & LOCATIONS

SCENE OUTLINE

SCENE
CHARACTERS
SETTING & LOCATIONS
SCENE OUTLINE

SCENE
CHARACTERS
SETTING & LOCATIONS
SCENE OUTLINE

SCENE

CHARACTERS

SETTING & LOCATIONS

SCENE OUTLINE

SCENE
CHARACTERS
SETTING & LOCATIONS
SCENE OUTLINE

SCENE

CHARACTERS

SETTING & LOCATIONS

SCENE OUTLINE

SCENE
CHARACTERS
SETTING & LOCATIONS
SCENE OUTLINE

SCENE

CHARACTERS

SETTING & LOCATIONS

SCENE OUTLINE

PART IV

THE FIRST DRAFT

IN THIS SECTION

WRITE THE FIRST DRAFT

Use the scene outlines from the previous pages to begin writing the first draft

THINGS TO CONSIDER WHEN WRITING THE FIRST DRAFT

- Don't worry about creating a perfect story the first attempt; write the rough draft and "perfect" the story later during the editing phase
- Writing a novel takes a long time, it can be helpful to make writing a part of your regular routine
- A great way to stay motivated when writing, is by tracking your progress whether by word count or by scenes written
- A tool that can be helpful when taking the information on the scene outlines and turning it into a written scene, is creating a zero draft - jotting down each part of the scene in point form to act as a clear path when writing

CREATE A WRITING ROUTINE

Consider when and where you plan to write, as well as steps you can take that will make your writing process easier

writing days and best time of day

things to do before sitting down to write

SCENE CHECKLIST

When writing each scene, consider the following elements:

- What is the goal of this scene?
- How does this scene connect to the greater story?
- What do we learn about the characters from this scene?
- Do the events of this scene logically follow the events of the last scene?
- Does this scene have a beginning, middle, and end?
- Does this scene effectively include:
  - Plot events that progress the story
  - Moments of character development
  - Realistic dialogue
  - Clearly grounding the reader in the setting
  - Use of the five senses for description
  - A consistent tone/mood throughout

OTHER THINGS TO TAKE NOTE OF

WORD COUNT TRACKER

Use this space to track your writing progress

WORD COUNT TRACKER

Use this space to track your writing progress

WRITING PROGRESS

Choose a word count goal and track your progress in the graph space below

TOTAL WORD GOAL

PROGRESS

DATE	WORDS	DATE	WORDS

WRITING GOALS

Keep yourself on track by creating writing goals

GOAL #1

STEPS OR MILESTONES

☐
☐
☐
☐
☐

TO REACH BY:

GOAL #2

STEPS OR MILESTONES

☐
☐
☐
☐
☐

TO REACH BY:

WRITING GOALS

GOAL #3

STEPS OR MILESTONES

- [ ]
- [ ]
- [ ]
- [ ]
- [ ]
- [ ]

TO REACH BY:

GOAL #4

STEPS OR MILESTONES

- [ ]
- [ ]
- [ ]
- [ ]
- [ ]
- [ ]

TO REACH BY:

STORY NOTES

STORY NOTES

STORY NOTES

STORY NOTES

STORY NOTES

STORY NOTES

STORY NOTES

For more writing help, follow us on **Instagram @darkgrovepress**

Don't forget to **leave a review** on Amazon to help other writers decide if The Novel Writing Blueprint will be useful to them on their writing journey!

For writing tips and freebies sent weekly to your inbox, join the **email newsletter** at **darkgrovepress.com**

Made in the USA
Las Vegas, NV
21 September 2023